Fold & Fly

BUTTERFLIES,
BIRDS, AND OTHER
ANIMALS THAT FLY

ROCK
POINT

Quarto Knows

Inspiring | Educating | Creating | Entertaining

Brimming with creative inspiration, how-to projects, and useful information to enrich your everyday life, Quarto Knows is a favorite destination for those pursuing their interests and passions. Visit our site and dig deeper with our books into your area of interest: Quarto Creates, Quarto Cooks, Quarto Homes, Quarto Lives, Quarto Drives, Quarto Explores, Quarto Gifts, or Quarto Kids.

First published in 2017 by Rock Point, an imprint of The Quarto Group,
142 West 36th Street, 4th Floor, New York, NY 10018, USA
T (212) 779-4972 F (212) 779-6058
www.QuartoKnows.com

Rock Point titles are also available at discount for retail, wholesale, promotional, and bulk purchase. For details, contact the Special Sales Manager by email at specialsales@quarto.com or by mail at The Quarto Group, Attn: Special Sales Manager, 401 Second Avenue North, Suite 310, Minneapolis, MN 55401, USA.

ISBN: 978-1-63106-296-4

Printed in China

5 7 9 10 8 6

Text by Stephanie Hoover
Engineering and illustration by Rob Wall
Additional illustration by Nuno Marques

Pterodactyl fold by Nick Robinson

Select photos are used with permission from:
Andre Helbig, Butterfly Hunter, Kirsanov Valeriy Vladimirovich, Kwirry, Panaiotidi, Sandhanakrishnan, Gyula Attila Hegedus, Ivan Kuzmin, Ondrej Prosicky, fpdress, Ana Gram, mark higgins, pandapaw, Catmando, Valentyna Chukhlyebova, Natalia Paklina, Daniel Huebner, davemhuntphotography, Ezume Images, Dennis W Donohue, Victor Tyakht, Madlen, Hintau Aliaksei, Darios, & Ultrashock / Shutterstock

This book is part of the FOLD & FLY BUTTERFLIES, BIRDS, AND OTHER ANIMALS THAT FLY boxed set and is not to be sold separately.

MIX
Paper from responsible sources
FSC® C017606
FSC
www.fsc.org

CONTENTS

Introduction...5

Insects: The First Flyers..............................6

Feathered Flight...10

Bats, Squirrels, and Lemurs...................18

Flying Fish, Frogs, and Lizards.............22

Lessons from Nature.............................24

Flight Control..26

Fold Instructions.....................................29

Guide to Folds...32

Guided-Fold Sheets...............................34

Butterfly and Flying Squirrel.................36

Condor...40

Macaw Parrot and Parakeet...................42

Bat...44

Kingfisher and Pterodactyl....................48

Hawk..54

Pelican...58

The Bird Fold..64

Mosquito..66

Dragonfly and Flying Fish....................68

Stork..70

INTRODUCTION

Human beings too often take for granted the miracle of flight. We barely notice the fat bumblebee floating from blossom to blossom, or the fireflies that briefly light an early summer evening. The silently gliding hawk and the bob-and-weave of the swallow go unappreciated. Even the perfect V-formations created by flocks of migrating geese escape our wonder. But they shouldn't. These seemingly effortless feats took millions of years to perfect.

Although we most associate flight with birds and insects, there are other surprising examples of flight in nature. Wings aren't the only requirement. Some furry creatures easily glide the length of half a football field. One amphibian species uses its parachute-like feet to travel amazing distances. Schools of a particular family of fish sail over the ocean's wave using abnormally large pectoral fins. Of course, man also "flies" with the aid of airplanes and helicopters—but it was only by studying flight in nature that human beings learned how to break the bounds of gravity and soar.

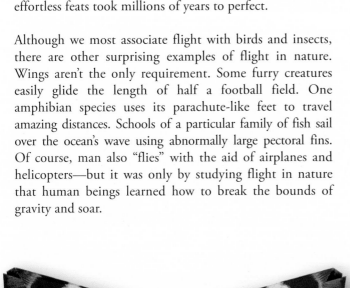

INSECTS: THE FIRST FLYERS

Insects existed in abundance long before other creatures joined them in flight. They began as earth or water dwellers. Either to catch food or to avoid being eaten themselves, they learned to jump. Evolution enhanced this ability by creating wings and strong muscles designed specifically for controlling them. Once acclimated to aerial navigation, insects migrated throughout the world. Some flew in swarms, others in pairs. All sought conditions best suited to their species' survival.

BUZZING AND BEATING

Nearly all insects have two sets of wings: forewings in the front, and hindwings to the rear. These wings are attached to the thorax, the part of the insect's body just behind its head. While one pair of wings remains stationary (helping to steer), the other pair vibrates rapidly. This vibration produces propulsion, the scientific term for movement.

There are insects that can fly with just one set of wings. The house fly is a common example. Mosquitos also have just one set of wings. They beat between 300 and 600 times per second.

The buzzing made by an approaching insect is actually the sound of air being fanned by its rapid wing movement. The smaller the wings, the more beats are required to fly. The more beats, the louder the sound. A honey bee, for instance, flutters its wings more than 190 times per second. By contrast, the large wings of butterfly can flap as few as nine times per second to maintain flight.

Most insect wings are transparent, resembling the leaves of plants. If you look closely, you can see they are filled with tiny lifelines: small veins carrying blood and oxygen. These tubes also extend inside the insect's body. When it's about to take flight, the tubes fill with air to help lift the insect, somewhat like a balloon being carried into the sky.

Unlike other flying creatures, insects have no backbone. To make up for this, the outer walls of the thorax are hardened to support its wings. While birds' wings narrow at the tip, insects' wings are small at the body and broad at the tip. Both the up and the down stroke require a great deal of energy but, when in flight, insects can reach speeds of between 5 and 90 miles per hour.

BEAUTIFUL SCALY WINGS

Butterflies and moths belong to the insect family known as Lepidoptera, which means "scaly wings." While their broad wings may look like one solid surface, they are actually made of thousands of tiny scales layered on top of one another like shingles on a roof.

Unlike bees or flies, butterflies are silent. Because their large wings require fewer beats, they don't disturb the air like smaller insects. There is no buzzing to alert you to their presence. They appear, almost magically, weaving up and down through flowers or over water.

The irregular flight line of butterflies is not accidental, nor are its vivid colors. The up-and-down motion makes it harder for birds and other predators to catch butterflies and moths. Meanwhile, the bright colors serve a number of purposes. Sometimes they allow the insect to blend into its environment and hide. Other times the colors are meant to convince predators that butterflies are bigger than they actually are. In some instances, their colors simply aid in keeping these cold-blooded creatures warm. The darker the wings, the more sunlight they absorb.

While it can be hard to distinguish butterflies from moths, their wings aid in identification. At rest, a moth's wings typically remain outstretched. Butterflies, on the other hand, hold their wings upright and together.

DRAGONS AND DAMSELS

Dragonflies were the largest prehistoric insects, in some instances reaching wingspans of more than two feet. Modern ancestors of these goliaths range from less than an inch up to six inches in length. Few other insects rival their beauty and speed.

The unusually long front wings of dragonflies make them easy to spot. They are often seen zigzagging across ponds or flower heads, occasionally stopping for a brief slumber on a blossom or blade of tall grass. Even though evolution urged them to leave their original water homes millions of years ago, dragonflies still return there to lay eggs. Once hatched, these offspring naturally take flight—no training required.

Closely related to dragonflies are damselflies. While very similar, there are two distinct differences between these species. Firstly, most damselflies are smaller than dragonflies. Secondly, unlike dragonflies whose wings are always extended, damselflies fold their wings against their bodies when at rest.

INSECT WINGS AREN'T JUST FOR FLYING

While wings are primarily for flight, insects have developed other uses for these appendages. On beetles, for instance, the forewings have evolved into hard shells offering protection from predators. Crickets have learned to make music with their wings. Honey bees have found, perhaps, the most ingenious uses. In the summer, when the hive is warm, honey bees beat their wings to push warm air out and draw cooler air in. In the winter, the beating of their wings produces body heat, warming the hive.

FEATHERED FLIGHT

What is often mistakenly considered the first bird was actually a flying reptile. Pterodactyls lived more than 150 million years ago. They ranged in size from animals small enough to fit in your hand, to beasts with wingspans of more than 40 feet.

Unlike birds, pterodactyl wings were made of a thin, skin membrane stretching from its fingers to its toes. Even the tail was covered. Yet even though pterodactyls were reptiles, they possessed some similarities to modern birds. The bones of Pterodactyls were predominantly hollow, allowing air to circulate. And their skeletons, though light, were able to withstand great strain. But contrary to what many believe, modern birds did not evolve from these meat-eating predators.

The sparrows, robins, and pigeons of today actually began as feathered, walking dinosaurs. One such creature, called the Archaeopteryx, is widely considered to be the true forefather of the birds that inhabit our skies. Ornithologists—scientists who study birds—believe it likely glided from one tree limb to another rather than achieving full flight. Either way, it is one of the earliest examples of an animal we would recognize as a bird.

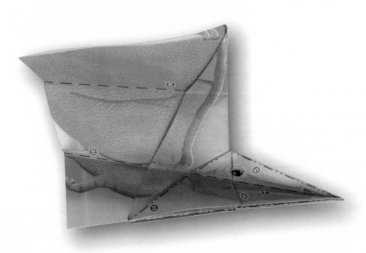

WE HAVE LIFTOFF

A bird's ability to take flight is its most astonishing skill. It is also its greatest challenge. First, the bird must make a running jump off the ground, or raise itself above the water's surface. When just high enough above land or water to fully flap its wings, the bird beats them up and down as rapidly as possible. By doing this, it creates its own breeze. As the wings push downward on this breeze, the bird's body rises skyward. It also gains speed. As the momentum increases, air flows over and under its wings creating a phenomenon known as "lift." It is lift that keeps the bird aloft. Upon reaching just the right altitude, it breaks free of gravity and propels itself by flapping, gliding or soaring.

Takeoff consumes more energy than any other activity. In fact, even if you don't see it, you know when a bird has taken flight. You can hear the rush of wind created by its wings as it surges skyward.

WINGING IT

Man is hard-pressed to create an engineering marvel as perfect as the wing of a bird. Although a bird's neck and spine are stiff and strong, the bones of the wing are incredibly light. Some of these bones are open at the wing's tip. This allows them to fill with air that eventually passes through to the lungs. Birds' tail feathers help execute mid-air turns, and also assist in slowing a bird's landing.

As you might suspect, the muscle attaching wings to the body is exceptionally strong. In some birds it accounts for half of the total weight.

Similar to the human arm, a bird's wing is jointed. The area above the elbow—the section attached to the bird's body—is covered in secondary feathers. The area below the elbow tapers to a point that, in humans, would be our fingers. This is where the primary feathers are found.

Most birds have ten primary feathers. Their job it is to propel the bird through the air. Secondary feathers keep the bird aloft. Their numbers vary greatly from species to species.

During molting, when old feathers are replaced by new ones, primary feathers are only lost two at a time. One feather on each wing falls out, and new ones grow in. Should a bird lose more than two primary feathers at one time, its ability to fly would be greatly diminished.

To better capture the wind, the section of the wing closest to the body is rounded, or concave. But, to prevent the wing from catching too much wind, the feathers yield and separate when necessary. Without this flexibility, a bird might be flipped over or pushed off balance.

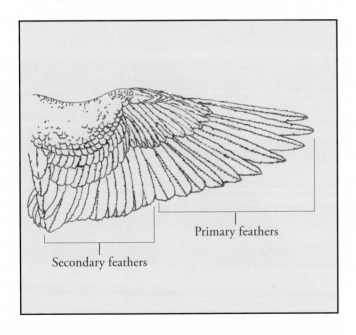

Primary feathers

Secondary feathers

To further allow wind to escape, the very tips of a bird's wings are pointed upward. This keeps the bird balanced, and prevents air from exerting more pressure against one wing than the other. Many airplanes employ this same design for the very same reasons.

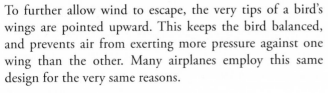

FLYING, GLIDING, AND SOARING

Once airborne, birds have three choices of movement: they can flap their wings to propel themselves forward, they can glide motionless with outstretched wings, or they soar upward by flying in circles. The choice depends both on the bird and its environment.

Birds with smaller wings must continuously flap to stay in the air. The tiny and speedy hummingbird, with a wingspan of only three or four inches, would fall to earth if it stopped beating its wings. Yet, unlike larger birds, it can lift off immediately, without hopping or taking a running start.

If you've ever tossed a paper airplane into the air, you already have an idea of how birds glide. There is no wing movement. The bird simply sails on air. The secret to successful gliding is wing size. Amazingly, the largest, heaviest birds are the best gliders. Storks, with their long legs, oversized beaks, and strange neck pouches, might look incapable of any kind of flying let alone graceful gliding. Surprisingly, though, they excel at this motionless flight, sometimes traveling great distances without so much as a quiver of their impressive, ten-foot wingspan. The White Albatross, whose wings spread nearly twelve feet, glides across the ocean for days. Working with air currents produced by waves, it conserves its energy until it absolutely must flap its wings to remain skyborne.

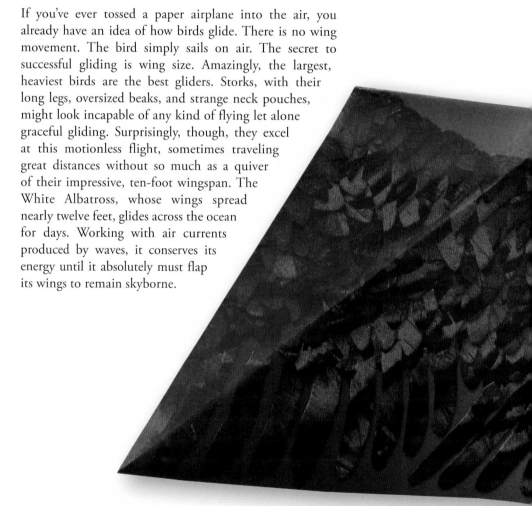

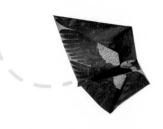

Of the three forms of flight, soaring is by far the most fascinating. To soar is to fly upward in circles, rising higher and higher in the sky with very little noticeable wing movement. Eagles, condors and hawks are all experts at soaring. They possess a unique understanding of how warm air rises, and they use it to their advantage.

The bird begins it circle by ascending on air rising from sun-heated roofs and other surfaces. To further gain lift and altitude, it turns directly into the wind. As the bird completes the circle, it eventually reaches a position where the wind is at its back. This provides momentum for the next revolution. On and on the bird circles, soaring to tremendous heights above mountains and cliffs.

Men have admired birds' ability to soar for centuries. Charles Darwin, while on a scientific voyage in 1839, wrote:

> When the condors in a flock are wheeling round and round any spot, their flight is beautiful. Except when they rise from the ground, I do not recollect to ever have seen one flap its wings... It was a beautiful spectacle thus to behold these great vultures hour after hour, without any apparent exertion, wheeling and gliding over mountain and river.

FLYING IN FORMATION

Many of us have seen airplanes fly in a V-shaped formation—but did you know that pilots learned this technique from birds?

When ducks or other migrating birds fly, they form a "V" configuration with one bird in the lead. Two birds fly behind the leader—one at each wing. A line of flock members forms behind each of these two birds, all slightly offset rather than in a straight line. Each successive bird encounters less pressure on its wings (a force known as "drag") than the bird in front of it. This is because the bird in front reduces the wind resistance for one behind it.

If birds flew in a direct line they would constantly fight one another's upwash—the air disturbance produced by flapping wings. This would consume too much energy. Instead, the birds fly just to the left or right of one another. Rather than hindering flight, this reduced air disturbance helps support a bird's weight as it flies.

Because leading the flock uses the most energy, migrating birds rotate this position. Older and weaker birds generally remain toward the rear of the "V" where resistance is weakest. Their natural instinct tells the flock that what is best for one bird is also best for them all.

COMING IN FOR A LANDING

Either to rest, feed or take care of their young, birds must at some point land back on earth. The process of stopping flight is equally as fascinating as taking off.

First, the bird spreads its wings as wide as it possibly can. This creates the drag necessary to slow down. At the same time, the bird points its body downward to navigate toward the ground. On nearing the landing spot, it drops its tail-end and lifts its head, all the while using its open wings to float gently earthward. Once on land, the bird often raises his wings above his head before tucking them neatly against his body. Ornithologists believe this may be similar to a human being stretching and relaxing their muscles after exercise.

VARIETY IN THE SKY

There are nearly 10,000 species of birds on planet earth. Each has its own habits, talents, and method of flight.

Some birds, like pelicans, are known by their incredibly large beaks and throat pouches. Much like a fisherman casting a net into the sea, the pelican skims the surface of the water gathering anything that looks like food. The excess water drains from its pouch, as it would through a net.

Wildly colored macaws are actually members of the parrot family. Their bright red, green, and yellow plumage helps them blend in with the leaves, fruits and flowers of their rainforest homes. Some macaws are small, like the parrots you might own or see in pet shops. Others stand up to 3-feet in height and can fly at speeds of 40 miles per hour.

There are birds that eat fish and crabs, and birds that subsist solely on seeds or fruit. From the tiny hummingbird no larger than some insects, to the ostrich standing more than nine-feet tall, each bird requires its own specialized menu. If humans truly "ate like birds," as the old cliche goes, we would likely be quite large indeed. Unlike us, a bird's metabolism is naturally lightning fast. It therefore must eat almost constantly to maintain the energy it needs to fly.

BATS, SQUIRRELS, AND LEMURS

Bats have a bad reputation. Perhaps it is their habit of flying at night in large colonies that frightens us. Or maybe it's all those old horror movies where the vampire escapes by transforming into one of these winged creatures and leaving through an open window. Whatever the reason, bats have been falsely cast as bad guys. In actuality, they are incredibly beneficial to humans—particularly in the summer when they eat tens of thousands of mosquitos.

By the time bats learned to fly, insects had been airborne for millions of years. This is no fluke of timing since bugs are bats' primary food source. Each evening when the sunlight fades, bats pour from their protected spaces to eat. A single bat can consume hundreds of insects per hour.

Like bees and other insects, bats also aid in pollination. Pollination is the process of fertilizing flowers and plants so they can create seeds. Without this, no new plants would grow.

Bats are the only mammals that can sustain flight for as long as they choose. They are found in nearly all parts of the world, except for very cold climates, or isolated locales. Like other mammals, bats are covered in fur and, when young, drink their mother's milk. They are born, like people; not hatched, like birds.

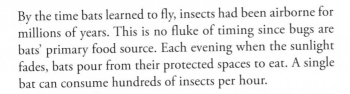

Nearly all of the bird species we know today already existed by the time bats developed the ability to fly. Unlike feathered creatures, bats' wings (like those of the pterodactyl) are covered by a thin membrane of skin. And unlike birds, which flap their entire wing during flight, bats use only the lower portion of their wing—a hinged section very similar to an outstretched human hand. One big difference, though, is that a bat's "hand" actually has more joints than ours does, making it capable of a wide variety of complex movements and adjustments while flying.

The great artist and inventor Leonardo da Vinci was fascinated with flight. He believed man needed only to mimic the motion of bats' and birds' wings to achieve it. In his notebooks, da Vinci proposed a contraption comprised of two large wings, strapped to his body, and controlled by his arms and legs. Like bats, these wings were to be crafted from a thin material stretched over a lightweight frame. There is nothing in his notes to suggest that da Vinci actually built or tested this invention, which is likely a very good thing. Though they looked like a bat's wings, da Vinci's proposed creations could not possibly have matched this mammal's natural capacity for flight.

While bats can remain in the air for an indefinite period of time, other mammals have developed an extremely accurate ability to glide from one perch to another of

their choosing. The nocturnal flying squirrel lives primarily in trees. When it wants to change locations, it climbs the tree trunk to attain the right height and then launches itself toward another tree. As it leaps, it spreads its arms and legs. Hidden beneath are large folds of skin that extend from wrists to ankles. Its bushy tail is completely exposed, perhaps to help navigate. Like a kite, the outstretched skin catches the air allowing the animal to sail fifty yards or more to its next stop.

Unlike their cousins the tree squirrels, flying squirrels rarely descend to the ground. Instead, they glide from branch to branch to escape predators and find the best food sources. Since they don't hibernate, just before winter flying squirrels fill their nests with enough food to survive the cold months.

Perhaps the most unique flying mammal is the flying lemur—although, in actuality, it is neither a lemur nor is it capable of true flight. Like flying squirrels, flying lemurs glide from place to place using a "skin parachute." Unlike flying squirrels, though, even a flying lemur's tail is encased in this skin.

Flying lemurs eat leaves, flowers, and plant shoots. During the day, they sleep in the most unusual fashion. Using all four paws, they hang upside down from a branch and tuck their head inside the pocket created by their skin. Passersby might mistake a napping flying lemur for a fuzzy, dangling piece of fruit.

FLYING FISH, FROGS, AND LIZARDS

We know that insects, birds and bats can fly. We also know that several species of mammals have developed amazing techniques for gliding. But did you know there are also water-dwellers that have found ways to fly?

Early ocean travelers were shocked (and sometimes frightened) to see hundreds of fish flying beside their ships using what looked like long, outstretched wings. We now know that flying fish, like squirrels and lemurs, don't actually take flight—they merely glide with the aid of ocean breezes and their extra-long pectoral fins.

When being chased by predators in the open seas, there are few options for escape. Flying fish have learned that the easiest method to evade swimming enemies is by doing what they can't. When chased, they naturally swim at top speed. This velocity, combined with a great thrashing of their tail fin, allows flying fish to thrust themselves skyward. Sometimes they get as high as four feet above the water's surface. Once airborne, it is not uncommon for them to travel 200 yards or more before returning to the sea.

While not as efficient as the large pectoral fins of flying fish, flying frogs use their unusual feet to glide. Like flying squirrels and flying lemurs, flying frogs live most of their life high in the trees where predators are easier to avoid, and food is easier to find. But unlike less talented amphibians that only swim or hop, the flying frog defies gravity. When jumping from branch to branch, all four feet spread open like umbrellas. These broad surfaces create air resistance. By leaning one direction or the other, the flying frog efficiently navigates to its target destination.

"Flying dragons" are not nearly as fearsome as they sound. Barely eight inches in length with a diet solely consisting of insects, these reptiles are no threat to humans. When climbing or sitting on a branch, the flying dragon looks very much like any other lizard. But when he needs to escape a hungry snake, or simply chooses to look for a meal, he springs from a tree branch into the air. Suddenly, the membranes attached to its ribs expand. Much like a superhero's cape, these membranes allow the flying lizard to complete a controlled glide to another tree, or all the way to the ground. Their only challenge comes from wind and rain, both of which prevent this lightweight creature from taking flight.

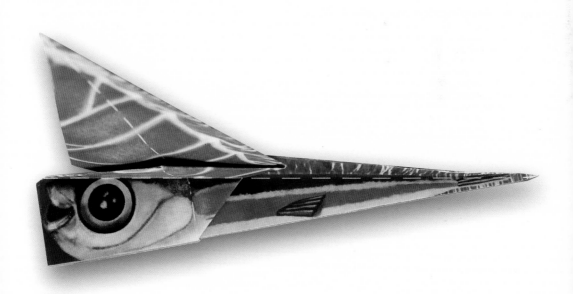

LESSONS FROM NATURE

Imagine the earliest man, watching creatures flying all around him and wondering how he too might one day join them. He didn't realize that all of the secrets to flight were right before his eyes. He needed only to study the insects, birds, mammals, fish and amphibians, for they had already solved this mystery.

The most important lesson nature's perfect flying machines teach us is that there is no "one way" to take to the sky. Whether by flapping feathered wings, soaring into the wind, or gliding with outstretched skin or feet, there are a multitude of ways to leave the ground.

Man eventually realized he would only ever fly as a passenger in a machine. People will, after all, never develop wings or air-filled bones. Still, the combined weight of a human and an aircraft convinced many we were simply too heavy to take flight. So, we continued to watch with wonder the birds and butterflies, dragonflies and flying fish. We continued to envy their ability to break free of the earth and carelessly sail the skies. And eventually, we too mastered flight.

On December 17, 1903, brothers Orville and Wilbur Wright made the first successful flights in a craft that not only weighed more than air, but also carried a human being. Their journey toward the manufacture of the airplane began by studying books about birds and insects.

The Wright brothers did not invent flight—nature had already done that for them. Instead, they created a way for us to do something we've dreamed of since the beginning of time: unburden ourselves from the pull of gravity and leave our worries below as we soar, like eagles, into the clouds.

FLIGHT CONTROL

We cannot, with inanimate paper, mimic the flapping wings of butterflies or birds—but we can replicate their ability to glide and soar. To do so, however, we must first understand the basic concepts of flight.

For these bird, insect and animal patterns to fly well, they must fly in a stable manner. In other words, they need to maintain their proper orientation in the air. We don't want our hawk flipping upside down or diving to the ground.

Roll

There are three forces that affect flight: roll, pitch, and yaw. Rolling is the familiar spin that airplanes, and even some birds, perform. It is achieved by lifting one wing until the entire body flips around horizontally. Pitch is created when the nose tips up or down. Yaw occurs when the body remains horizontal while turning to the left or right.

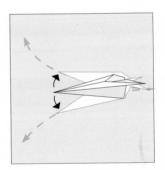

Each of these forces is affected by a particular characteristic of the wings. Small adjustments meant to create flight stability are called "trimming the plane." Trimming is more art than science, and the best way to learn is to experiment to see what works. The following tips should help.

Pitch

If your flying creature rolls over into a spiral, then bending both wings upward slightly from horizontal will help stabilize it. If the nose tips down so that the plane dives to the ground when it is thrown, then bending the back edge of both wings up slightly will provide more lift and correct that dive. If the nose tips up too much so that your bird or insect goes straight up and stalls or flips over, then bending the back edges of the wings down slightly will correct that and level out the flight. It is rare for a paper creation to fly in such a way that it yaws, but if that were to happen, bending the rear vertical section to the opposite direction will straighten it out.

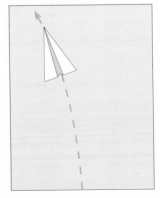

Yaw

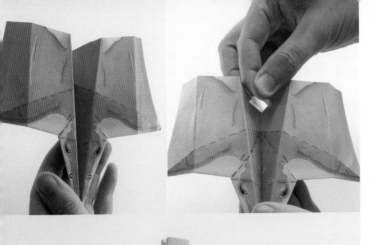

> You'll find some of the more complex folds spring open, which can impair their flight. Feel free to tape the edges together for a more stable plane.

> Bend the wings up slightly for more stable flight. If they're uneven, the plane will roll.

> Bending the back edge of the wings upward will cause the plane to climb, or just keep the nose up. Bending them down will cause the nose to drop.

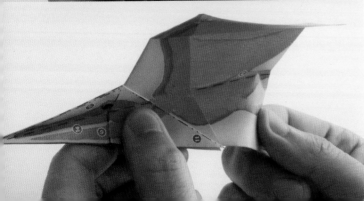

> Adjust the rear vertical edge to compensate for yaw.

Now that we've learned how to make our creatures fly in a straight line, how do we purposely get them to do tricks? The same principles can be applied to encourage rather than prevent roll, pitch, or yaw. To make a turn, the axis must tilt. In other words, it must roll slightly in the direction of the desired turn. The lift provided by the wings will be pointed slightly into the direction of that turn, with the result being that the body will move in a curve in that direction. The stronger the lift, the tighter the turn. For many of our designs, this can be accomplished by simply tilting the creature to the desired side during launch. If you want a tighter turn, trim it to give it more lift, by bending the back edges of the wings up a bit.

Paper plane tilted to turn

In order for your bird or insect make a loop, the nose must pitch upward as it flies. If the nose continually pitches upward, your bat or dragonfly will climb and eventually turn upside-down and continue to fly along that circle until it is flying level again. For some flying creatures this looping comes naturally. They have large wings compared to their body size, and a center of gravity that is closer to the center of pressure. To adjust the trim so your creature will loop, raise the nose by increasing the lift. Bend the rear of each wing slightly upward, but bend the edges more, so that it is overcorrected. Additionally, you must throw a bit harder than normal so that the speed creates enough lift to pull your creature up and over into a loop.

FOLD
INSTRUCTIONS

Paper-crafted flying machines and creatures have fueled the centuries-long human desire to explore flight. This brief overview provided a taste of the science behind this aeronautic magic. The following pages will teach you how to fold some insects, birds and animals of your own, so you can take to the skies!

GUIDE TO FOLDS:

The following pages have instructions for 12 different folds. Understanding the symbols here will make folding a breeze.

VALLEY FOLD: fold forward

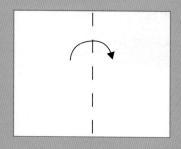 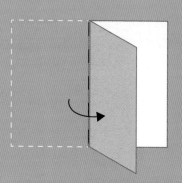

MOUNTAIN FOLD: fold backward

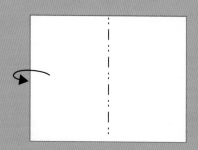 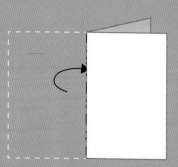

CREASE: from a previous fold

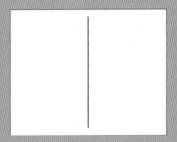

FOLD & UNFOLD: fold and then unfold to create a crease

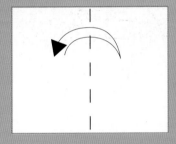

INVERT: create creases and push corner or edge in along folds

*Only one fold line is shown, but for best results,
 crease both forward and backward.

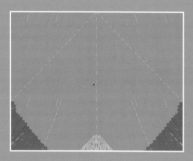 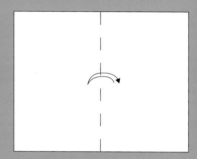

MATCHING PATTERNS:

An image of the corresponding patterns appears at the beginning of each fold instruction. Align the paper as shown in the first instruction to match the final fold.

RED FOLDS & BLUE CREASES:

Full folds are labeled with RED numbers.
Creases are labeled with BLUE numbers.

SIMULTANEOUS FOLDS:

Some steps will cover 2 or more folds. Each of which will be labeled with the step's number on the sheet.

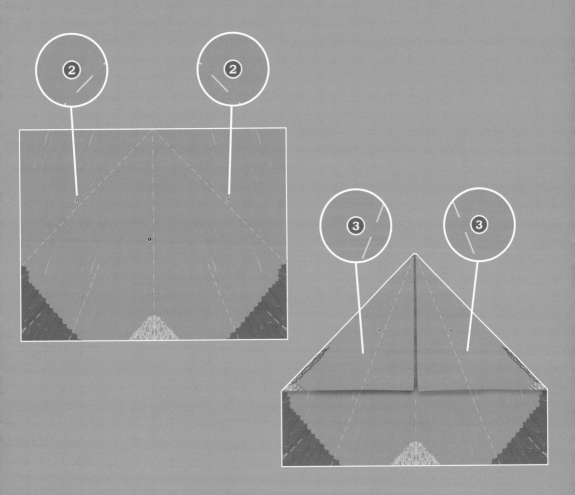

UPRIGHT NUMBERS:

The numbers should appear upright when the paper is aligned with the directions.

BUTTERFLY AND FLYING SQUIRREL

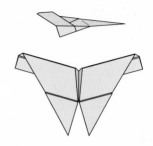

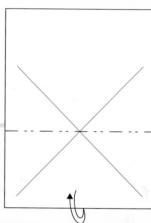

1

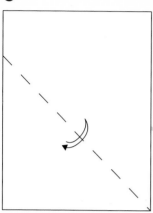

Create a crease by folding the bottom edge up diagonally to align with the right edge.

2

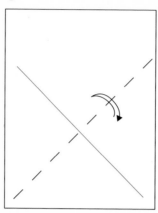

Create another crease by folding the bottom edge up diagonally to align with the left edge.

3

Create a horizontal crease through the crossing point of the diagonal creases.

10

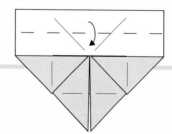

Fold the top edge down as shown.

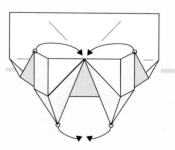

continued on page 38...

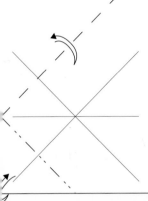

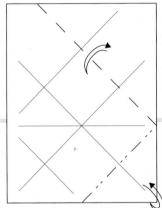
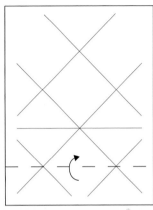

4

Create creases by folding the left side over to align with the horizontal fold.

5

Create creases by folding the right side over to align with the horizontal fold.

6

Fold the bottom edge up to the horizontal crease.

9

Fold the top corners of the front flap down and to the center as shown.

8

Fold hoizontally through the crossing point of the diagonal folds to bring the back fold to the front.

7

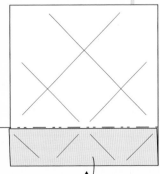

Fold the bottom backward along the horizontal crease.

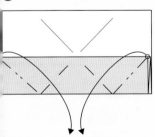

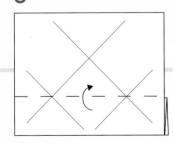

...continued from page 36

11

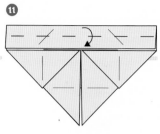

Fold the top portion in half again.

12

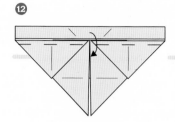

Fold the top edge down one final time, including a portion of the bottom folded area.

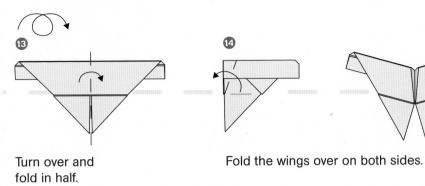

Turn over and
fold in half.

Fold the wings over on both sides.

CONDOR

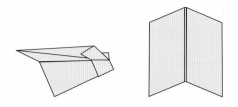

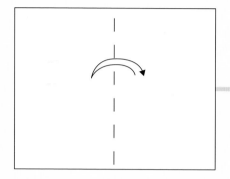

❶

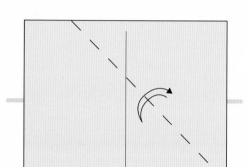

Make crease by folding in half.

❷

Make crease by folding the right edge down to the bottom edge.

❽

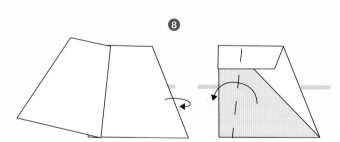

Fold both wings over to complete.

❼

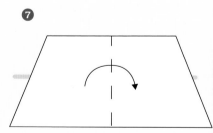

Turn over and fold in half.

3

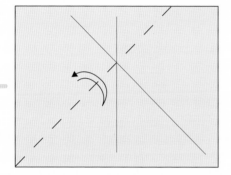

Make crease by folding the left
edge down to the bottom edge.

4

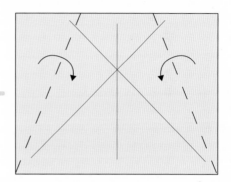

Fold left and right sides over
to align with diagonal creases.

6

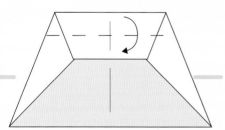

Fold top down again.

5

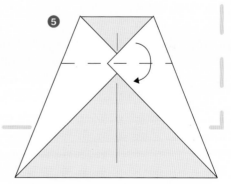

Fold top down as shown.

MACAW PARROT AND PARAKEET

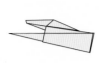

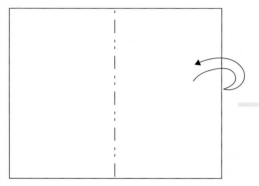

❶

Make crease by folding in half.

❷

Fold top corners down to the center crease.

3

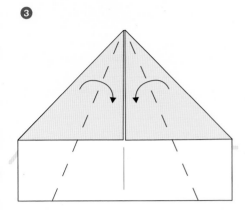

Fold top edge of outer folds to the center crease.

4

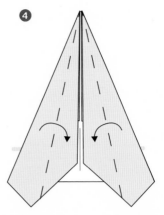

Fold top edge of outer folds to the center crease again.

6

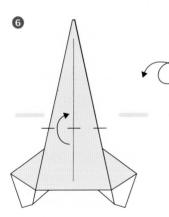

Turn over and fold the bottom portion up at the top point of last fold.

5

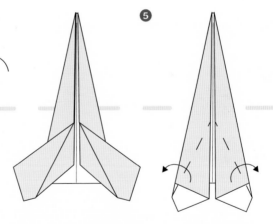

Fold bottom flaps back outwards as shown.

7

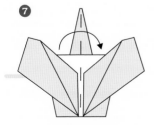

Fold in half along center crease.

8

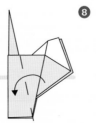

Fold wings down on both sides to complete.

BAT

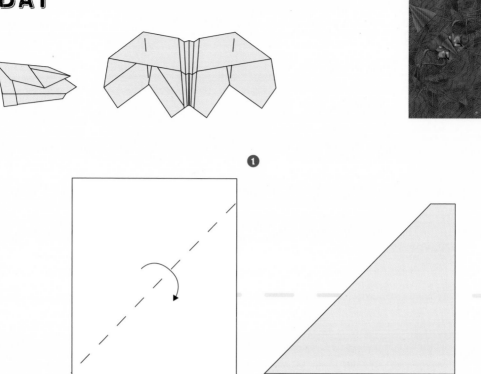

1

Fold diagonally, so equal lengths of paper extend off the bottom and right sides.

4

Fold the top edge down.

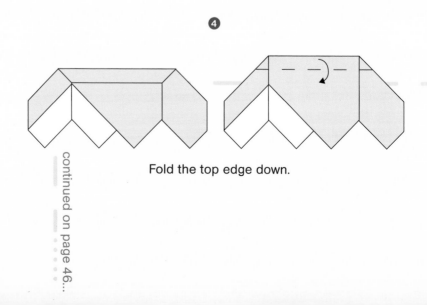

continued on page 46...

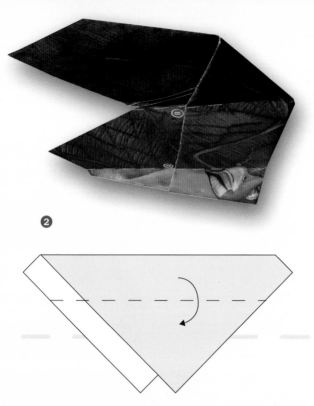

②

Rotate as shown and fold the top edge down.

③

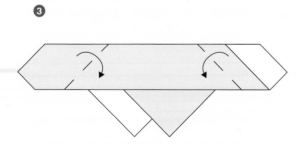

Fold the outside points down to create
four level points along the bottom.

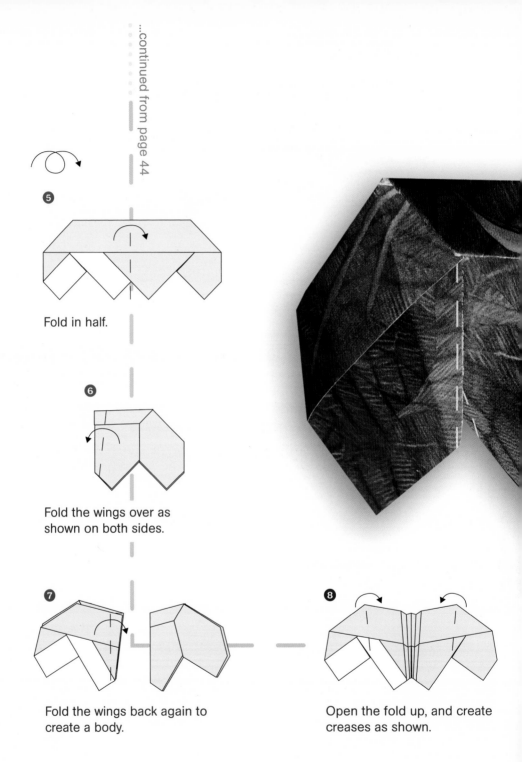

...continued from page 44

5

Fold in half.

6

Fold the wings over as shown on both sides.

7

Fold the wings back again to create a body.

8

Open the fold up, and create creases as shown.

KINGFISHER AND PTERODACTYL

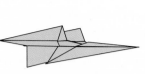

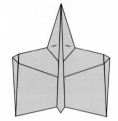

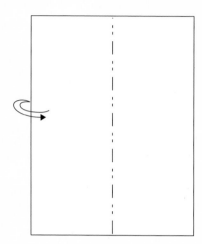

Fold in half.

❷

Create creases at 1/4 the
width of the page by folding
the sides ot the center crease.

❻

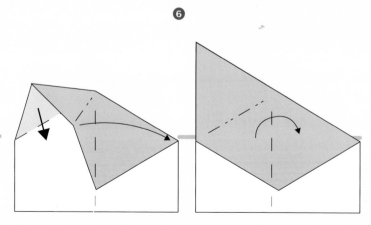

Fold the left point of the flap over to the right side as shown.

continued on page 50...

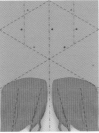

3

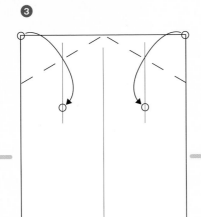

Fold top corners down to
the 1/4 width creases.

5

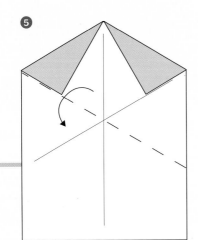

Fold the top right portion down
along the edge of the right flap.

4

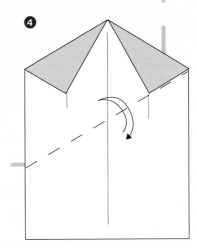

Create a crease by folding the
top left portion down along the
edge of the right flap.

7

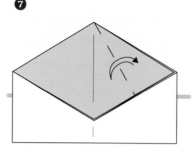

Create a crease by folding
the top of the right flap
down to the center crease,
both forward and backward.

8

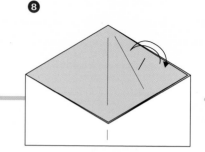

Create another crease by
folding the right point of the
flap up to the top point.

11

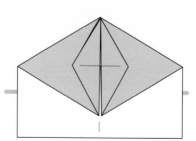

Use the creases you've
created to fold the bottom
point of the top flap upward
and flatten as shown.

continued on page 52...

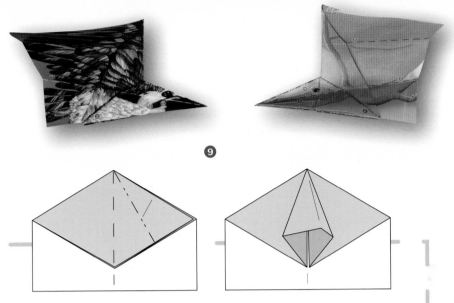

9

Use the creases you've created to
flatten the top flap as shown.

10

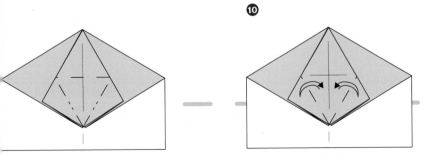

Create creases by bringing
the side points of the top
flap to the center crease,
both forward and backward.

...continued from page 50

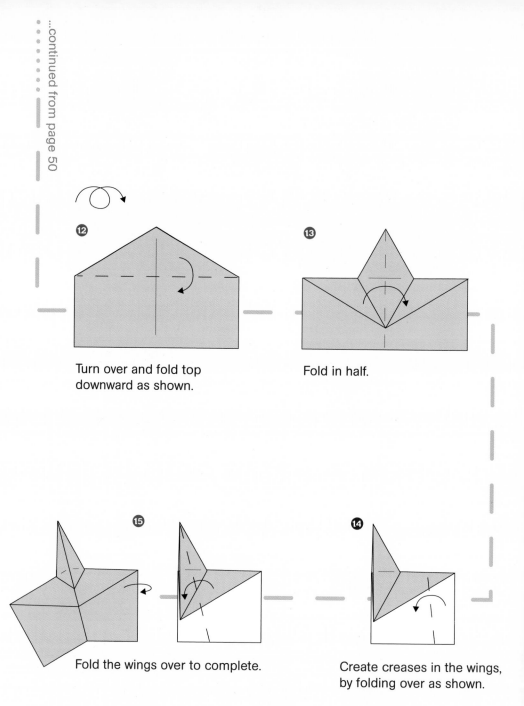

⑫ Turn over and fold top downward as shown.

⑬ Fold in half.

⑮ Fold the wings over to complete.

⑭ Create creases in the wings, by folding over as shown.

HAWK

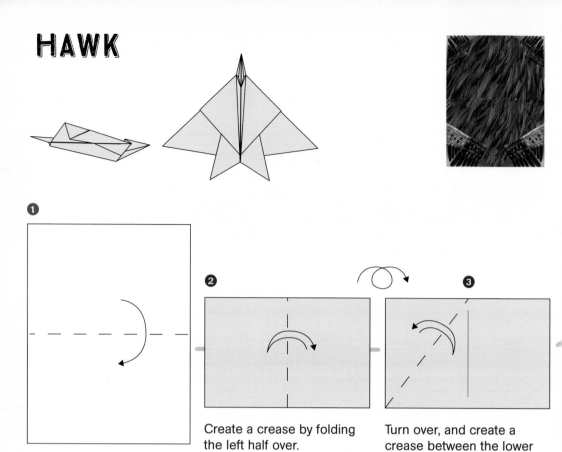

1

Fold the top half down.

2

Create a crease by folding the left half over.

3

Turn over, and create a crease between the lower left corner and the center of the top edge.

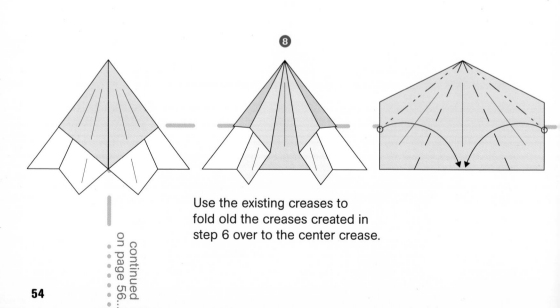

8

Use the existing creases to fold old the creases created in step 6 over to the center crease.

continued on page 56...

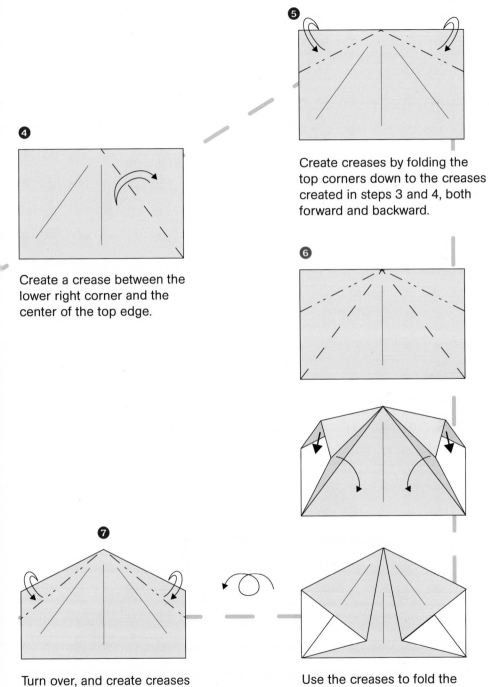

Create a crease between the lower right corner and the center of the top edge.

Create creases by folding the top corners down to the creases created in steps 3 and 4, both forward and backward.

Turn over, and create creases by folding the top edges down to the existing crease.

Use the creases to fold the right side fo the front flap downard, keeping the right side of the back flap in place.

...continued from page 54

9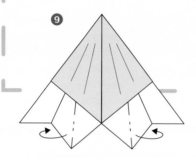

Fold the right side of the middle flaps backward, so the outer lower edge aligns with the inner lower edge.

10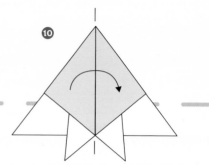

Fold in half.

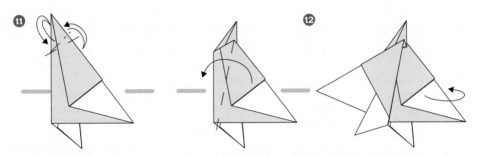

⑪ Create creases as shown, and invert the top point.

⑫ Fold the wings over to complete.

PELICAN

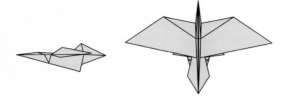

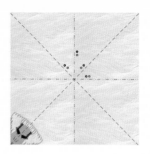

❶

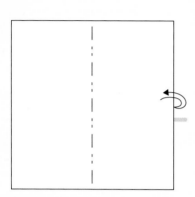

Create a crease by folding the right half back.

❷

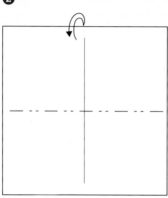

Create another crease by folding the top half back.

❸

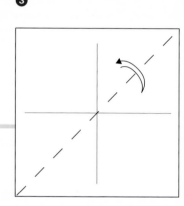

Create another crease by folding the top left corner down to the lower right.

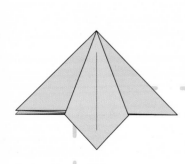

❼

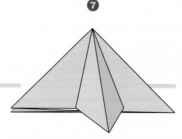

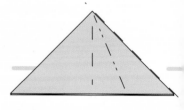

Use the existing creases to fold the right edge down to the center, while flattening the flap with the creases created in step 6.

continued on page 60...

④

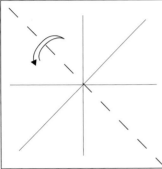

Create another crease by folding the top right corner down to the lower left.

⑤

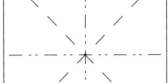

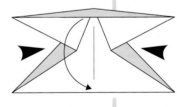

⑥

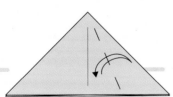

Create a crease by folding the right edge over to the center crease, both forwards and backwards.

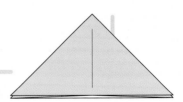

Use the existing creases to bring the top half down, while inverting the sides.

...continued from page 58

8

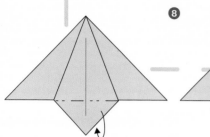
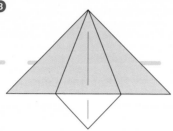

Fold the forward bottom
flap backwards and tuck
into the pocket in the fold.

9

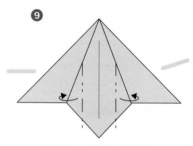

Fold the sides of the
forward flap backward,
to the center crease.

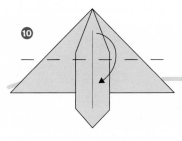

10 Fold the top edge down as shown.

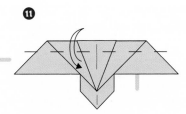

11 Create a crease by folding the top flap upward as shown.

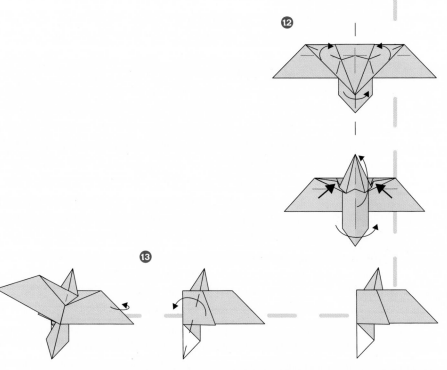

12

13 Fold the wings and tail over as shown to complete.

Fold the bottom edge of the top flap up to the top edge as shown. At the same time, fold the entire piece in half, inverting the top flap point.

THE BIRD FOLD

The mosquito, dragonfly, flying fish, and stork fold all start with the classic origami bird base, shown here.

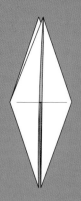

❶

Create a crease by folding the top half back.

❷

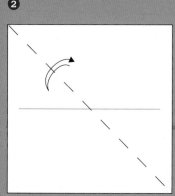

Create a crease by folding the top right corner down to the lower left.

❸

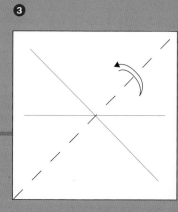

Create another crease by folding the top left corner down to the lower right.

❼

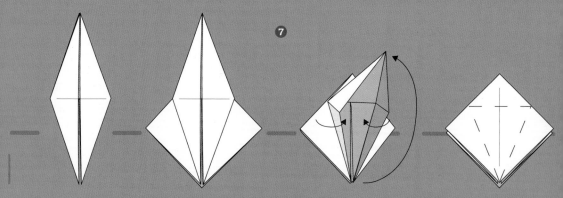

Use the creases created in step 6 to fold the bottom point upward and flatten. Complete on both sides.

Continued on pages 66 (Mosquito), 68 (Dragonfly and Flying Fish), and 70 (Stork).

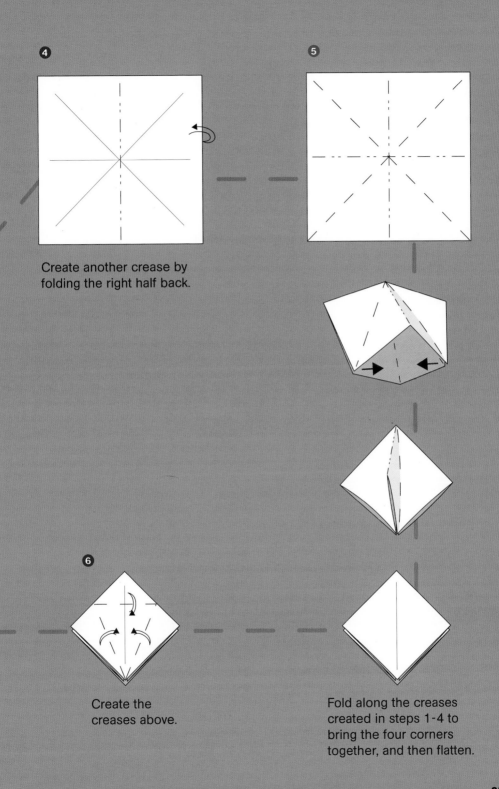

4

Create another crease by folding the right half back.

5

6

Create the creases above.

Fold along the creases created in steps 1-4 to bring the four corners together, and then flatten.

MOSQUITO

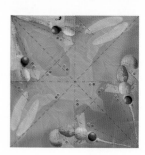

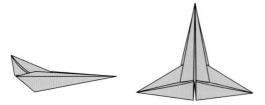

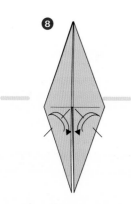

8

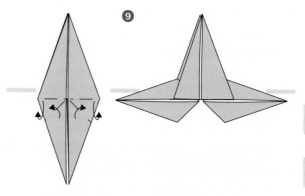

9

Create creases by folding the bottom flaps out at a 90° angle, as shown.

Using the existing creases, fold the bottom flaps up at a 90° angle, inverting one half, so it tucks inside the top fold.

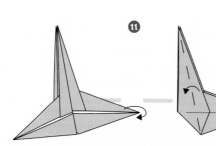

11

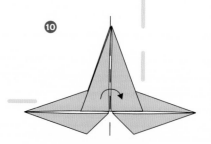

10

Fold out wings to complete.

Fold in half.

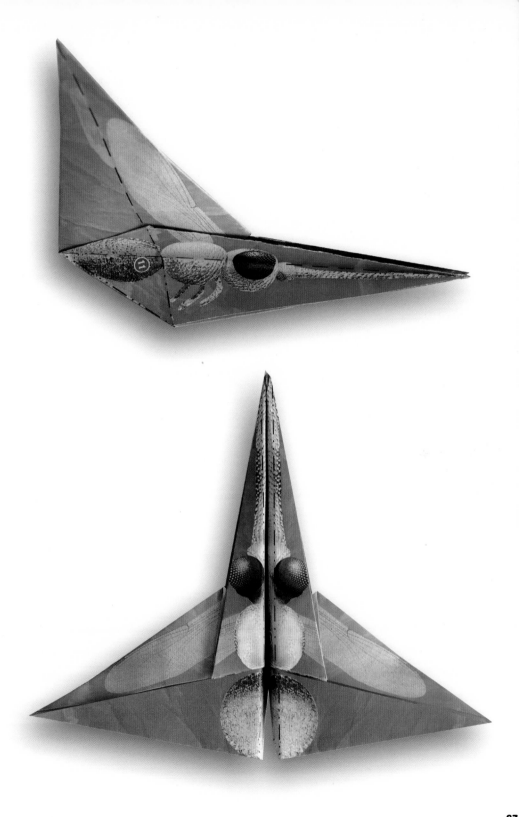

DRAGONFLY AND FLYING FISH

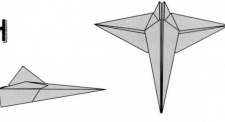

8

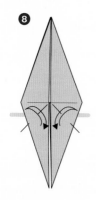

Create creases by folding the bottom flaps out at a 90° angle, as shown.

9

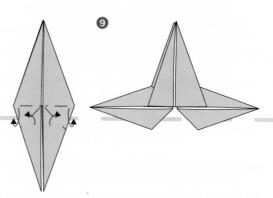

Using the existing creases, fold the bottom flaps up at a 90° angle, inverting one half, so it tucks inside the top fold.

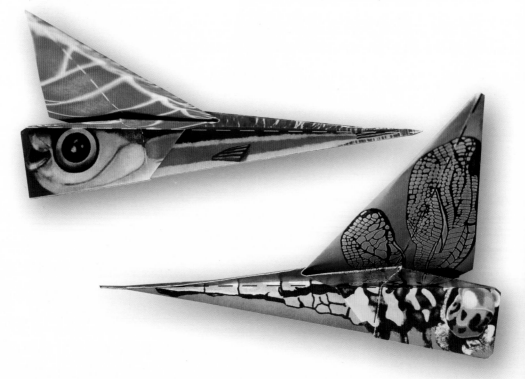

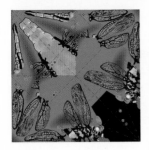

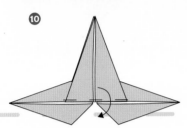
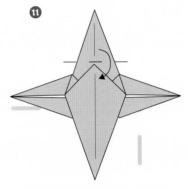

10

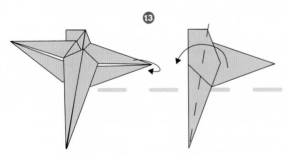

Fold the front flap down along the existing crease.

11

Fold the top of the back flap down, over the tip of the forward flap.

13

Fold the outside edge over to the center fold, creating the wings.

12

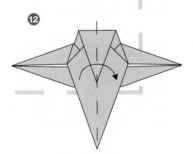

Fold in half.

STORK

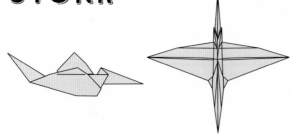

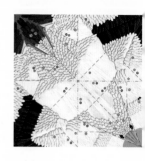

8

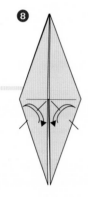

Create creases by folding the bottom flaps out at a 90° angle, as shown.

9

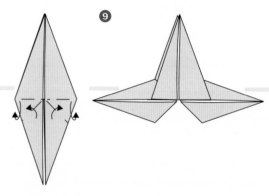

Using the existing creases, fold the bottom flaps up at a 90° angle, inverting one half, so it tucks inside the top fold.

14

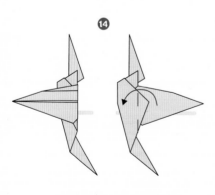

Fold the wings over on both sides to complete.

13

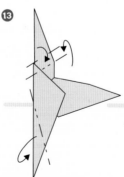

Create creases and invert the top and bottom points to create a head and tail.

12

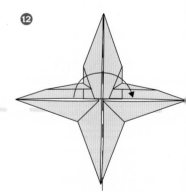

Fold in half

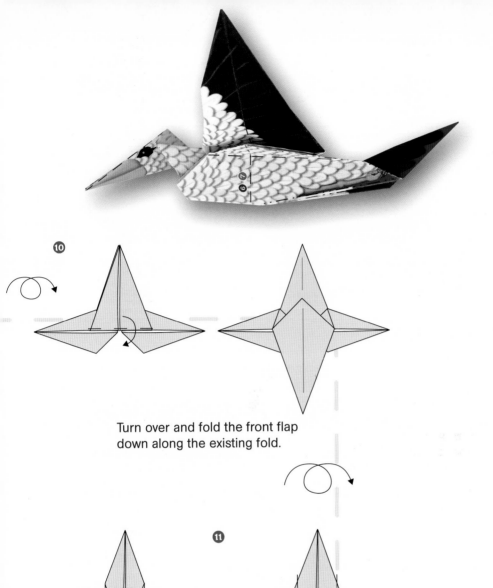

10

Turn over and fold the front flap
down along the existing fold.

11

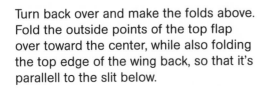

Turn back over and make the folds above.
Fold the outside points of the top flap
over toward the center, while also folding
the top edge of the wing back, so that it's
parallell to the slit below.